For Sandy.
Love you, girlfriend!

This book is a work of fiction. Names, characters, businesses, places, events, locales, and incidents are either the products of the author's imagination or used in a fictitious manner. Any resemblance to actual persons or animals, living or dead, or actual events is purely coincidental.

We welcome you to include brief quotations in a review. If you would like to reproduce, store, or transmit the publication in whole or in part, please obtain written permission from the publisher. Otherwise, please do not store this publication in a retrieval system. Please do not transmit in any form or by any means electronic, mechanical, printing, photocopying, recording, or otherwise. Please honor our copyright! For permissions: Contact MindView Press via email: mindviewpress@gmail.com

Published by MindView Press: Hibou

Author: Andi Cann

Illustrator: Zuzana Svobodová

The Chicken who Thought She was a Bat
ISBN-13: 978-1-949761-73-3 eBook
ISBN-13: 978-1-949761-61-0 Paperback
ISBN-13: 978-1-949761-62-7 Hardback
ISBN-13: 978-1-949761-67-2 Audio

Copyright©2020 by Andrea L. Kamenca. All rights reserved.

the CHICKEN who thought she was a BAT

written by **ANDI CANN**

illustrated by ZUZANA SVOBODOVÁ

"Bye, Mama. I'm going to play with Git Yer and Lang."

"Ok, honey, I hear we're getting a new neighbor in the coop next door. Be on the lookout!"

Git Yer and MerryLyn walked down to the creek and then back to the neighborcoop. They saw a young chick in front of the new coop with many, many feathers on her head. They ran toward her waving excitedly.

"Hey! Hey! Do you want to be friends? Do you want to do chicken or goat or lizard stuff together?"

Popsy was **terrified.**

She turned around and ran into her coop. Then, she peeked out the window at them.

Later that day, Mama asked MerryLyn, "Did you meet the new neighbor?"

"No, Mama, she just squawked and ran into the house."

"Oh, dear," said Mama Chicken. "Perhaps you should try again tomorrow when it's just you."

The next day MerryLyn went over to the coop and knocked on the door.

When it opened, the same chicken peeked out from behind it.

"Hi! I'm MerryLyn! I'm the chicken next door. I used to think I was a goat, but that's another story. Aaannyywwayy...do you want to be friends?"

"Yikes!" The door slammed, and MerryLyn heard some muffled sounds. A mama chicken opened the door and said, "Hi, MerryLyn. Popsy is very shy..."

MerryLyn heard someone say, "And tell her!"

The mama chicken sighed and said, "And Popsy thinks she's a bat."

Popsy jumped out.

"I don't just think I'm a bat!

I AM A BAT!

I have two wings, just like a bat."

MerryLyn looked from the mama chicken to the baby chick, shook her head, and said, "I have two wings.

I'M NOT A BAT!"

The days went by, and sometimes the Critter Creek Farm animals would see Popsy peeking out from her coop window, but as soon as they waved, she disappeared. Mama Chicken talked with Popsy's Mama and learned that Popsy was shy. So, the two of them hatched a plan.

Early one morning Mama Chicken and Popsy's Mama told both MerryLyn and Popsy to go see Don Key Hotey and ask him if Popsy was a bat. Git Yer decided to tag along. When they got there, MerryLyn blurted out, "Mr. Key Hotey, is Popsy a bat?"

Mr. Key Hotey eyed the two of them, "Well, it looks like the two of you are up with the chickens...Oh, ahem, ahem, you ARE chickens. Now, have the two of you flown the coop? Hmmm, no, that's not right.

Neither one of you are bad eggs, right? No, that's not it. Well, here's the feet and feathers of it all. You're both chickens. You live next coop to one another. Be friends. The end. And, that's the hard-boiled truth."

Popsy protested and said, "I am NOT a chicken. I AM A BAT!"

Mr. Key Hotey looked at Git Yer and shook his head, "Not this again." Mr. Key Hotey then sighed, looked Popsy up and down, and said in his very wise voice, "Go to the windy hill. There you will find out if you are a bat. On the way there, take at least three friends and explain why you are a bat." Popsy blinked and agreed.

The next day Git Yer, MerryLyn, Popsy, and the Professor trekked down the path, past the creek, over the knoll, through the woods, and up to the windy hill. Git Yer asked, "Why do you think you're a bat again?"

Popsy said, "I have two wings. I'm black. I sleep during the day (Well, not all the time!) Actually, I never do. But, still, I'm BLIND AS A BAT! ... I can't see!"

When they got up to the windy hill, Popsy stood on top of Git Yer. The wind blew back her feathers. She shrieked! "I can see. I can see!"

Git Yer chuckled. It seems that Popsy's feathers were so unique, so long, so fluffy, she couldn't see past them. Then, Git Yer had an udderly fantastic idea.

He talked to the Professor who flew away and came back with a little stick. Then, Max, the spider (who had hitched a ride on Git Yer) spun the stick in Popsy's feathers away from her eyes.

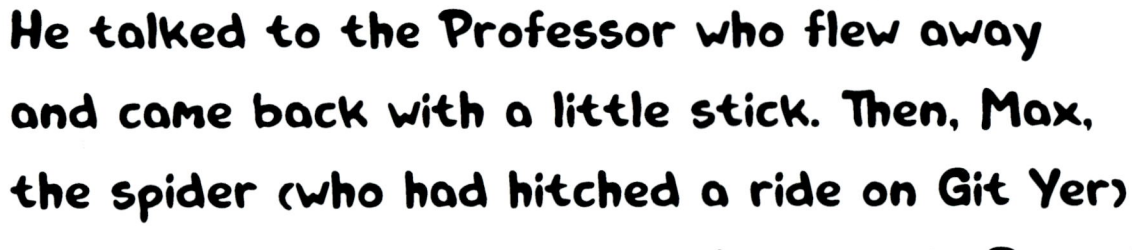

Then, they all hoofed it home. It was easier now that Popsy could see.

Popsy burst into her coop and said, "Mama, Mama! Guess what?

I'm not a bat! I'm a CHICKEN!

Popsy's Mama caught the eye of MerryLyn's Mama and smiled, "Wonderful! I was walking on eggshells, but now that you know you're a chicken, shake a tail feather, and go do your chicken chores!"

Popsy groaned but grinned and said, "Thanks, MerryLyn, for being my friend. Being a bat wasn't everything it was cracked up to be!"
MerryLyn giggled.

"See you tomorrow, Popsy!"

Dear Reader,

I hope you enjoyed the adventures of Popsy and MerryLyn. Aren't they an adorable bunch? Can I ask you a quick favor? Would you leave a review? It helps other readers and me! I read all of them. Thank you! And, I love connecting with readers. If you register your email address on my website https://www.andicann.com, you will receive a free gift and be the first to know about new books, special offers, and free gifts!

Thank you!
Andi

If you liked this book, you might like some of my others, too!

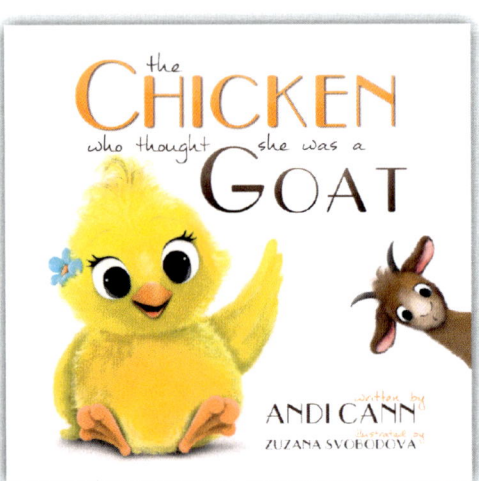

Made in the USA
Coppell, TX
05 August 2020

32557715R00021